MW00323800

I Survived Childhood: A Memoir of Abandonment, Betrayal, and Healing

By Hyun Martin
and Linda Kenyon

Book Cover by Nicole Bresner
Book Layout by Marie-Estelle Pham

Book cover designed by Nicole Breslin. Book layout designed by Marie-Estelle Pham.

Be You Spa Inc.
PO Box 83052
Gaithersburg, MD 20883
www.hyunmartin.com
(301) 493-4911

Ordering Information:
Quantity sales. Special discounts are available on quantity purchases by corporations, associations, and others. For details, contact the publisher at the address above.
Printed in the United States of America

Publisher's Cataloging-in-Publication data
Martin, Hyun
I Survived Childhood : A Memoir of Abandonment, Betrayal and Healing / Hyun Martin ; with Linda Kenyon
p. 102
ISBN 978-1-947235-00-7
1. The main category of the book — Memoir. 2. Self Help — From one perspective. 3. Mind, Body, Spirit — And their modifiers. I. Martin, Hyun II. I Survived Childhood: A Memoir of Abandonment, Betrayal and Healing

First Edition

This book is for Brian, Cameron and Sean. I am so grateful for your love and support.

Thank you, Carla and David. Thank you, Steve and Janice.

To immigrants, adoptees, people of color and survivors of rape and incest: May we all speak out and protect the next generation. May we strive to change the culture of silence, shame, blame and guilt in our lifetimes. Let's work together to shine light on injustice and domestic violence for children, women and men and may we work together to create a more just and compassionate world!

Acknowledgments

It takes a village! To all my friends, clients and family that have had to put up with my crazy years between 2015 till now. Thank you for your support, shoulders, and love. I believe that I don't compartmentalize my life. I am who I am. I appreciate my clients that gave me some normalcy in my grief while caring for two sets of parents in decline and the deaths of two fathers.

Thank you, Evelyn Maier for your poem, Broken Child! It was the perfect beginning to the book.

Thanks, Teres and Michael Wright for your support when things were spiraling and work was a safe place. to be.

Bob Rodman, Laura Lipson and Karen Kulgren who did some edits and suggestions in the early drafts of the book.

Laura Cagle for being there in Lampasas, Killeen, Mexico and Austin. Thank goodness for Facebook.

To my brother, Jin Bowden for reading and remembering our childhood that was horrific and brutal for both of us. Thank you for giving me your support throughout our lives. I hope that you feel loved and appreciated by your little sister.

Thank you, Ayda Sanver, my immigrant "sister" for understanding cultural differences, for all your advocacy work for autism and for telling me about Tree House Child Advocacy Center of Montgomery County. Meeting Tom Grazio and Nina Blecher gave me a reason to get my story out, so I could help change things for the abused children of Montgomery County and nationwide.

To my writing partner and "sister," Linda Kenyon, we were at a point in our lives where we could share our gifts with each other for over one year of Friday night healings and Saturday night writings. Our different abilities complimented each other. I would not have made this story as coherent and well written as it is without your guidance. You helped to pare down what was relevant and what was not while editing my life into nine chapters.

Sharing our childhoods, narcissistic mothers and our lack of validation bonded us as sisters. Ohana is family and while I still have a birth and adoptive family. I choose you and Ayda as sisters of my heart. We get to share, laugh, cry, dance and make art together as orphans.

My children, Cameron and Sean have not had to experience sexual abuse, but your childhoods were not trauma free. I hope you will always know what is important in life. Love to you always and may you receive and give love freely to the world.

To my partner, husband and best friend for much of the 27 years we have known each other. I love you and treasure the connection and sense of belonging that I feel with you. You know all my flaws and still continue to love me and understand and support me. Thank you for creating family from the ashes of our childhoods and continuing to be a rock for our family.

To you the reader, I hope that you find that inviolable piece of your soul/spirit and reclaim your innocence and worth as you read this book. I hope you share with the world your pain and allow others and yourself to heal from creating a safe space filled with wisdom, compassion and understanding. To thine own self Be True!

Hyun

I was born a perfect child ...

—Hyun Sook Jung

I Survived Childhood: A Memoir of my Journey to Overcome Abandonment and Betrayal

By Hyun Martin

When I was three years old my mother thought she was dying and gave me up for adoption. She gave me to her sister and her sister's husband. That was my first major trauma.....

Maternal Family Tree

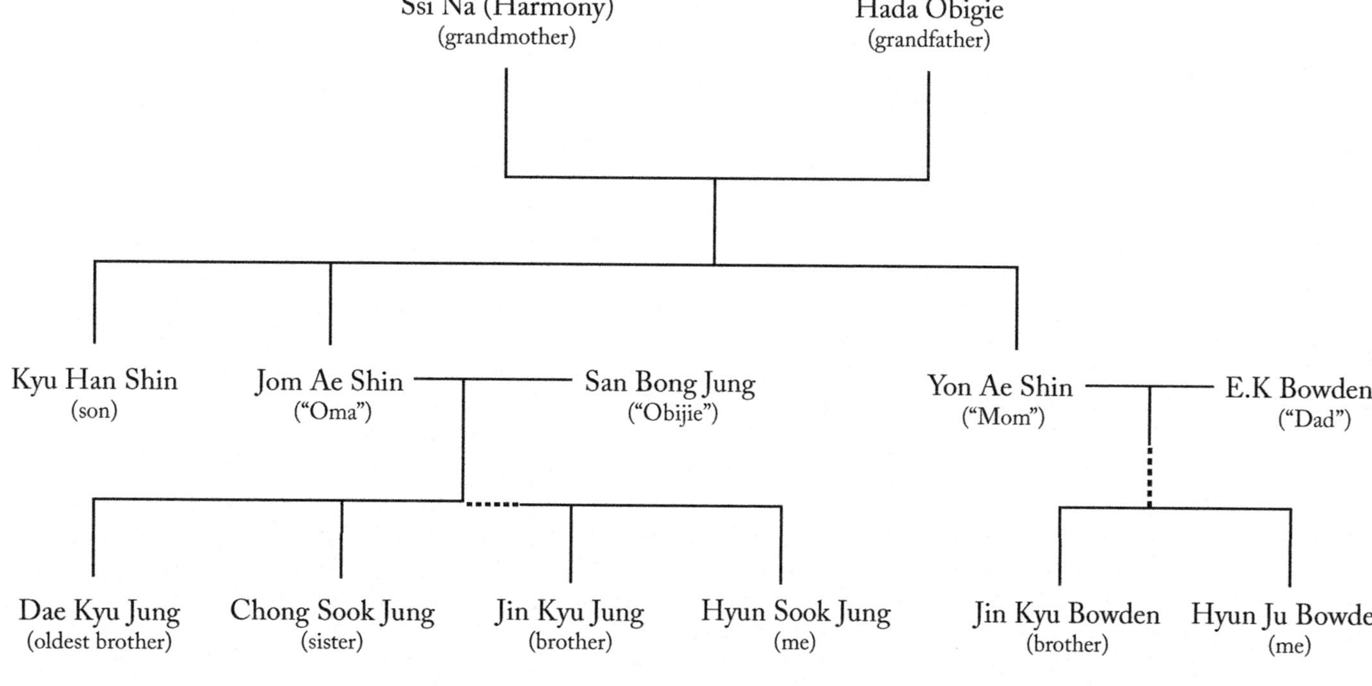

Broken Child

By Evelyn Maier

Robbed of her innocence and childhood
No one to turn to, No end in sight
Alone, she did the best she could
Although, it seemed a futile fight
At a very young age
She learned how to survive
It was the only way to stay alive
Her mind just simply, instinctively
Went away
That's how she coped
Day after day
Now years have passed
However, she still harbors
The pain and the sadness
Days pass by
But time stands still
I can no longer deny
It's taking over
Against my will
Maybe I'm embarking
on a journey
to insanity

At first it was easy to hide
Considering I had no idea
What was lurking inside
The broken pieces of a shattered child
Has begun to emerge
Splintered and wild
It's hard to decide
Which is worse
The cause or the effect
or
Forever living the curse

Introduction

This is a book about rising above one of life's greatest challenges and showing that adversity can either make you stronger or leave you weak and broken. I've found a way to become stronger. I hope, for the countless number of children out there who have experienced sexual abuse, they will be able find a way to rise above it and become stronger too.

Child survivors of sexual abuse are especially strong and in many ways more resilient than others. They have experienced multiple forms of trauma at a young age. They've also experienced a disruption in caregiving; some may have been raised by a grandparent, a foster parent, or an older sibling. The younger they are when they experience this disruption, the more their development is derailed.

Sometimes, their disruption in caregiving was because the caregiver himself or herself was the abuser.

This aspect of the development of abuse victims is clinically documented and scientifically annotated by Joyanna L. Silberg in her book The Child Survivor: Healing Developmental Trauma and Dissociation.

Abuse can define you if you let it. It wasn't until I was in my '50s that I realized this and was finally able to speak out about it. I hope that in doing so I will inspire others to realize that abuse does not define them. My hope is that if we all look out for each other and speak out about abuse, we can break down the barriers that have allowed abuse to continue unabated and in shockingly high numbers.

To be sure, there will be triggers that will arise in your life that will take you back to that dark place you would much rather forget about; but if you find a path to the light you will come out the other side. You also will be able to help others break the cycle of abuse. My greatest hope is that this book will help you do that.

In childhood, the need for touch is intrinsic, but safe touch is not always given. In adulthood, we take our learned behaviors and past experience, our fears and our rules for appropriate interaction to become a safe touch-deprived society. I want to change this dynamic and show that there is appropriate and safe touch. Much like we needed it in childhood, we need it in all stages of life.

Hyun Martin (May 2017)

Seoul, South Korea 1963
Oma, Myself, and Mom (aunt/mom)

Table of Contents

1

I was three years old. My mother, Oma, was ill and poor. She and my father, Obigie, were struggling to raise a family in post-war Korea. It was a difficult time for them. Oma thought she was dying. She didn't explain to me at the time why she thought she was dying but she did tell me a few things later in life, when we became reacquainted.

She said because of her poor health she was afraid Obigie would remarry and I would end up with an evil stepmother. To save me, she explained, and as an ultimate act of love and sacrifice, she decided to give me up to her sister and her sister's husband who had no children of their own. They became my Mom and Dad in what was to become the start of a years-long ordeal.

Two-thousand-842 Days, 68-thousand-208 Hours, Four-million-92-thousand-480 Seconds: I did the math; that's how long I lived with the fear that I would be abandoned and discarded again. There is no way to describe the terror of my life. I was living with a madman with his own demons. He took advantage of a child's trust, he betrayed and abused that trust by utilizing my body for his sexual pleasure. He took away my childhood and my ability to choose what I wanted for myself. His behavior destroyed my innocence, my self-respect and self-esteem and led me to self-destructive behavior during my teenage years.

My older brother was eventually 'given up as well and turned over to my new Mom and Dad. We became puppets in a puppet show of my Dad's choosing. Whether it was one of his drunken binges or acts of rage and violence, he was bigger than us and he commanded fear. He was, to me, the "blue-eyed devil" of my life. He made my body respond to sexual stimulation way too early for me to even understand what was happening to me. I had no say in the matter. I was simply his plaything for sex.

Moving to America

I was only four-and-a-half years old when I was sent to America. I don't remember much about Korea, or Inchon, where we lived, except one thing: I remember watching people planting seeds in the fields when I was two-and-a-half years old. With each and every hole they dug, they would drop in fertilizer, and then the seeds. I was told this was the best fertilizer you could possibly use. I thought, if it was so good, it must also taste good! So I reached into a hole, pulled out some fertilizer, and ate it. It did not taste good! It tasted horrible! That's probably because the fertilizer was

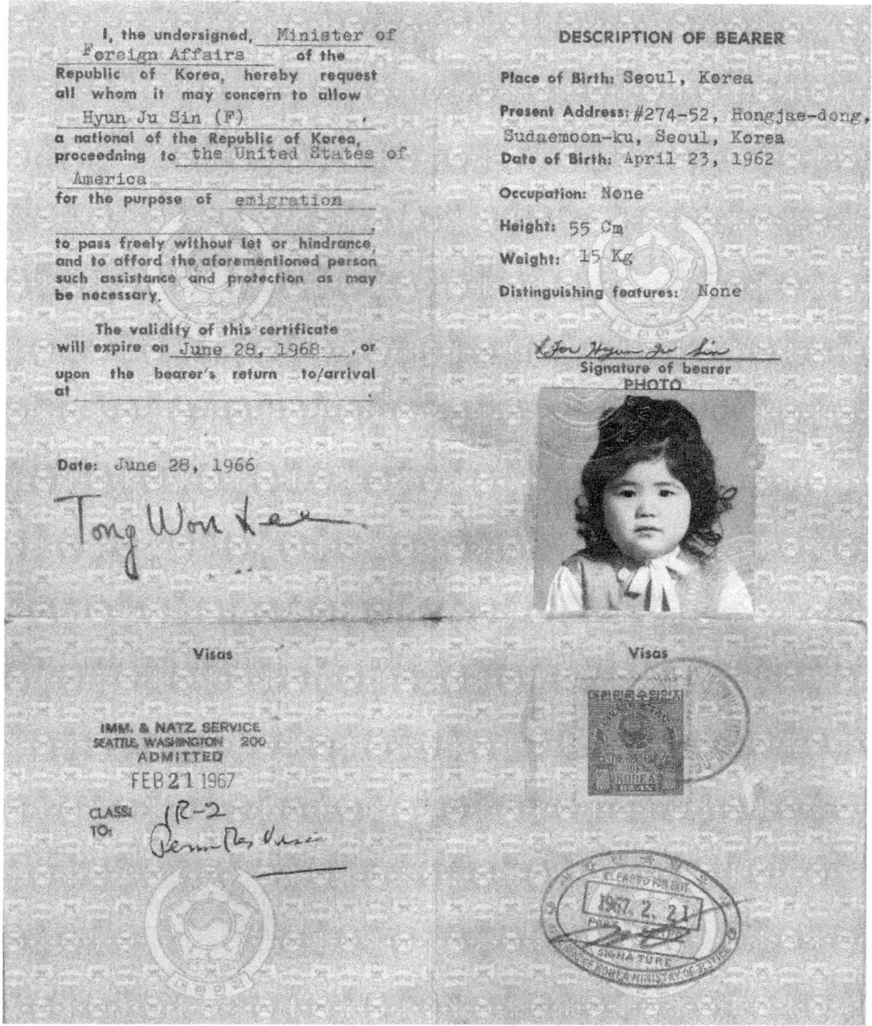

I, the undersigned, Minister of Foreign Affairs of the Republic of Korea, hereby request all whom it may concern to allow Hyun Ju Sin (F), a national of the Republic of Korea, proceedning to the United States of America for the purpose of emigration, to pass freely without let or hindrance, and to afford the aforementioned person such assistance and protection as may be necessary.

The validity of this certificate will expire on June 28, 1968, or upon the bearer's return to/arrival at .

Date: June 28, 1966

DESCRIPTION OF BEARER

Place of Birth: Seoul, Korea

Present Address: #274-52, Hongjae-dong, Sudaemoon-ku, Seoul, Korea

Date of Birth: April 23, 1962

Occupation: None

Height: 55 Cm

Weight: 15 Kg

Distinguishing features: None

Signature of bearer

PHOTO

Visas

IMM. & NATZ. SERVICE
SEATTLE, WASHINGTON 200
ADMITTED
FEB 21 1967
CLASS: IR-2
TO:

Visas

KOREA

CLEARED FOR EXIT
1967. 2. 21
SIGNATURE
KOREA MINISTRY OF JUSTICE

Travel Certificate of the Republic of Korea

really chicken shit. I remember more than anything else that everyone was laughing at me as I spit it out. I was embarrassed and humiliated.

I learned a powerful lesson that day: No matter what, "don't be humiliated." From that day on I watched people very carefully. I studied them. Since I was a good little girl, I tried desperately never to be humiliated, embarrassed, or shamed ever again. This was an early lesson in my life: "Never bring shame to the family." Later, but not much later, I became a victim of sexual abuse. I was the one humiliated, embarrassed, and shamed, but I learned to keep it to myself and to 'never bring shame upon the family.' I learned to be quiet, obedient and above all, "appropriate."

This culture of silence that was drummed into me is a common theme among sexual abuse victims. It is also a destructive, insidious affirmation that the behavior perpetrated upon victims of sexual abuse is somehow "okay" as long as no one talks about it. It took me almost 50 years to break my silence. I am not ashamed about what happened to me anymore. My adoptive father, the man who was supposed to protect me as my real father might have done, should be the one who was humiliated, embarrassed, and ashamed: Not me.

2

Rejoining the Story of my Childhood

My real mother and father had six children. I was the youngest. My Oma, Jom Ae Jung and my Obigie, San Bong Jung, gave me up for adoption. Mom had lost two children after they were born; she also suffered a number of miscarriages. By the time I was born, 15 years after my oldest sibling, Oma simply couldn't cope anymore. She gave me and my brother Jin to my aunt, Yong Ae Shin, who couldn't have any children of her own.

My aunt had married a white American serviceman stationed in Korea, whom she met while working at the local Korean store. His name was E.K. Bowden Jr., or Edward Kara Bowden, Jr. He became my new father and my worst nightmare.

I was born Hyun Sook Jung. My new name became Hyun Ju Bowden. I wouldn't see my real parents again until I was 10 years old. It was a bizarre, bewildering, confusing encounter that occurred when they came to America to live with my older sister in Galveston, Texas. Up until then I had blanked them out; I truly didn't remember them at all.

While still waiting for my brother's adoption papers to come through, and before my brother and I were able to leave Korea for America, I was placed in the U.S. Military Hospital for much-needed eye surgery. I suffered from a common affliction among Asians: Our eyelashes can grow straight up into our eyes, and must be surgically corrected by stitching along the lid to re-direct the lashes. My real parents left me with my Aunt who dropped me off and then left me, at the age of three, at the military hospital for the surgery. My real parents didn't even say goodbye. I didn't know, at the time, that I wouldn't see them again for many years.

I didn't know what was happening to me at the hospital. I couldn't speak English; no one at the hospital could speak Korean. My eyes were bandaged after the surgery so I couldn't see. I was frightened, alone among strangers, and helpless.

When I was released from the hospital, I went to a strange home that was not my own. It was a Korean home in Seoul, not Inchon, where my real parents lived. It was the home of my new parents, my aunt and uncle. From that moment on, I was to call my aunt "Mom." My uncle became "Dad," although everyone

E.K. and Yong on their western wedding day in South Korea 1963.

E.K. and Yong on their Korean Royal Wedding in South Korea 1963.

else called him E.K.

My brother Jin and I lived in Seoul, where E.K. was stationed. He stayed mostly at the barracks while we lived with Mom in a more traditional Korean home. We were there for about a year and a half. My real grandmother lived with us. She was my biggest source of comfort, but when I left for America, I didn't see her again for many years, either.

The Korean home in Seoul had heated floors because life in Korea was lived on the floor. The floors were heated by little fires that warmed up stones placed underneath. We sat, slept, ate, and did everything on the floor.

There was also an outhouse. The Korean people used this multi-family outhouse that had gaps between the wooden slats. It was drafty and dark and I was terrified to go in there! I kept imagining falling through the hole, never to be seen again. It smelled nasty!

When I was four and a half, my brother's adoption papers came through. This is when E.K. and Mom moved us to the US. I flew on Pan Am with E.K. My Mom flew on a separate flight with my brother Jin. I don't know why we were separated. I barely knew this man E.K. I didn't speak English. He didn't speak Korean. He had to care for me, a frightened little girl who kept throwing up during the flight. E.K. didn't know what he was doing. He certainly didn't know how to comfort me and certainly had no idea how to be a parent.

We moved into a trailer park at Fort Hood, Texas. It was 1967. There was a diverse community of military families at this trailer park. Our neighbors included an Okinawan family and a Filipino family. They were Asian, although not Korean, and I never felt out of place or "foreign." Six months later we moved to the small town of Florence, Texas. I remember the sign as you entered the town that said "Population 675." I know this because I learned to read and speak English in Florence and I never forgot the sign.

And So It Begins

In America E.K. did not allow any of us to speak Korean in the home. Over time, I forgot my native language. I remember saying to my brother: "Jin, I don't remember a word of Korean. What's the word for candy?" "Sartang," he said. Jin remembered Korean because he was six years older than me and had had more time to learn the Korean language and culture than I did.

I was five years old when the abuse started. We had some major storms in Florence and in a trailer home you can feel every gust of wind and every drop of rain. It frightened me. E.K. started coming into my room to "comfort" me. He would come into my bed and tell me to hold his "thumb." Soon, this became a nightly ritual. He liked this, and he especially liked that I was such a good little girl and did what I was told. Of course, it wasn't his "thumb" at all, it was his penis. I knew it wasn't his thumb, but I didn't want to get in trouble by saying anything. I didn't want to be embarrassed or humiliated. I just wanted to be a "good girl."

E.K. soon moved us again, this time to Lampasas, Texas, population around 5000. I was eight. Once again I was torn from my familiar surroundings. I felt isolated, separated from my friends and from everything I knew. This made me feel lonely and especially vulnerable.

E.K. retired from the military in 1969. He had been in the Army at least 18 years. At retirement he was able to collect a full pension.

"Our Little Secret"

I was eight years old and E.K was still coming to my room to "comfort me." Then he started fondling me. He penetrated me for the first time when I was nine, and I became a rape victim. E.K. told me this was to be "Our Little Secret." He told me not to tell anyone. I knew it was wrong, but I didn't want to be embarrassed or humiliated if I said anything. I certainly didn't want to get in trouble. I did as I was told and kept the whole thing "Our Little Secret."

No One to Protect Me

I don't know if Mom knew what was going on. Over the years, I have come to believe that she did know about it for quite some time but she didn't do anything about it. She didn't want to bring "shame" upon the family by acknowledging it. I also think she was probably frightened of E.K. and did not have the courage to confront him.

Every aspect of her life was controlled by E.K. She was prohibited from speaking Korean, prohibited from eating Korean food, prohibited from observing her native culture. When E.K. left to serve two tours of duty in Vietnam, she was able to be herself and was much more fun with Jin and me. We ate dried squid, kimchi, and other foods E.K. prohibited, food he had called "smelly" and banned from the home. When he came home from Vietnam Mom reverted back to that quiet, obedient, Korean woman he required her to be. But her silence, and "appropriate" behavior actually made her complicit in the abuse that was perpetrated against me.

The Saturday Routine

Starting when I was eight years old, E.K would send my brother out to the barn to milk the cows and feed the horses. When he was done he came back inside and we all had breakfast together as a family. After breakfast, my brother was sent back outside to finish his chores which included mucking out the stalls and exercising the horses. Mom went into town to do her shopping. She was gone at least two hours. My grandmother was sent outside to tend the chickens.

This routine left me alone with E.K. every Saturday morning. He would sit me down on the couch, fondle me, and say he was "developing my breasts." He called them my "titties." He would stimulate me between my legs using his penis, until he would "come" on my stomach. Afterward I was told to vacuum, clean the bathroom, and dust the living room. By the time I was nine years old, I had breasts; probably a B cup. That's when he started to rape me. He told me "don't worry, it will only hurt the first time."

3

True Confessions

When I was ten years old, my mom's friend, Key, came to visit. She stayed with us for one week. During her visit she was able to observe the family dynamic. She told my mom "something is going on between E.K. and Hyun that is "not normal." She voiced her suspicion that E.K. was molesting me.

She may have thought it was strange that my brother shared a bedroom with our grandmother. My brother's room had two twin beds. My room had one double bed and was the furthest away from my parents' bedroom.

Years later, both my brother and I discussed this and agreed that this arrangement gave E.K. the access to me that he wanted. No one questioned it at the time because we were "good kids" we were "nice" and we were "compliant." Mom probably didn't want to stir up any trouble if she, if fact, thought this was somewhat wrong. The fact that E.K. disappeared into my room every night for at least 30 minutes didn't prompt her to speak out either.

In retrospect, it must have taken a lot of courage for Key to say something to my mom. It wasn't until two years after that conversation that Mom responded. One day she drove me to the parking lot at my middle school and asked me if E.K. had done anything with me sexually. I said "yes." She said "don't tell anybody." She added "if it ever happens again, it's all your fault." Of course, it happened again. Of course I didn't tell anyone.

Within a couple of days of my conversation with Mom when she told me to keep quiet, E.K. confronted me. He said "I got into a lot of trouble! Don't talk about this! Keep quiet! This is our secret!" He scared me. So I kept my quiet.

Be Quiet, Ke Quiet

Ke Quiet! Be Quiet! Keep Quiet!

My step mother would say, "Ke quiet!"
It wasn't until I was nine and
I lost an argument with a classmate
That "Ke quiet!" was not a word in the dictionary.

Five was when I was scared by lightening.
The thunder would reverberate in the trailer house that we lived in.
My stepfather would come into my bedroom.
He would say, "Be quiet! Hold onto my thumb."
Only it wasn't his thumb. It was his penis.

Nine was the same time that I lost my virginity.
I was penetrated vaginally by my stepfather.
I said, "It hurts!"
My stepfather would say, "Keep quiet!"

So I learned to float away.
I learned to dissociate from reality.

Now at 52, I am learning that my childhood was torture.
I am finally examining my life and examining my fractured selves.

I am working to become whole for my innocence was taken away from me.
I am working on reclaiming my innocence.

I am angry and sad and go back and forth like a pinball.
I am angry not only for myself, but for all abused children.

I am no longer keeping quiet!
I am speaking up and speaking out.
I am ready to roar with my truth and feel my feelings.
I allow myself the space and time to process my feelings.
I am a Pillar of Light connected to the center of Earth and the center of our Sun!
I am a Divine child of God as you are also a Divine child of God!
This is my truth and universal truth.
We are all a part of the Divine!
Help me be in the Joy of Connection and Peace.

Myself at 13 years old 1975.

My Real Parents Show Up

I was about to turn ten years old and my life was turned upside down again. One day while I was in the kitchen, the door opened and in walked a Korean couple. They were my real parents! I had blocked them from my memory. I only knew they were my parents because my Mom told me they were. Truly, you could have put any two Korean people in front of me and told me they were my parents and I would have believed you.

I had had zero communication with my birth parents over the past seven years. If my Mom corresponded with them, I was never informed about it. My birth parents were completely erased from my world. The shock of seeing this woman who was supposedly my real mother cannot be adequately described in words.

I had no idea why these people were even here!

Galveston

About two weeks after I "met" my birth parents they took me with them to Galveston, Texas to visit my sister. She was 22 years old--12 years older than me. I had only met my sister for the first time the previous year, so she, too, was pretty much a stranger to me. My sister's name is Chong Sook Chung, but she Americanized it when she became a U.S. citizen and became Elizabeth Sook Chung. Since she spoke English she acted as the translator between my parents and myself because they only spoke Korean; I only spoke English.

I spent the summer with my sister and my parents at the home of her U.S sponsor, Mr. Earl Weeks. She required a sponsor in order to come to America, get a green card and a student visa. My sister had worked for Mr. Weeks in South Korea. He was one of the engineers who helped design the Korean subway. In America, Mr. Weeks paid for my sister's college education in Galveston. She eventually got her Bachelor's degree in nursing. My birth parents paid for her Masters and PhD. at the University of Texas in Austin.

My visit to Galveston became a magical time for my family and me. We spent almost two months together at Mr. Weeks's home. Obigie got up early every morning, walked to the beach and gathered beach towels left there the night before. He would then go to the boats and help the fishermen unload their catch. Obigie would then come home with the towels left on the beach and seafood the fishermen had given him for his help. We didn't have much money but we did have good food.

At night we would play Hotto, a Korean card game. Although my parents had been strangers to me, we were getting to know each other. They were actually fun to be with. This was the first time in my life that I felt my parents and my sister loved me. I was happy!

At the end of the summer the moment I always dreaded finally came: I was sent back to Lampasas, to E.K.'s house because my parents remained behind in Galveston.

Escape from Galveston

I never quite understood what happened but from what I've been able to gather, my father and Mr. Weeks did not get along. Either he threw my parents out or they decided to leave on their own and they ended up back in Lampasas where they rented a house. I didn't live with them. I remained at E.K's house, but I did see them on weekends. It wasn't until about a year later that I moved in with my birth parents. I was 11 years old.

Obigie worked as a laborer at a feed mill in Lampasas. His job was to load and stack bags of feed and he did so each and every day, at least eight hours a day, without complaint. If he could work overtime, he did. Oma cleaned houses. Between the two of them, they saved up enough money to buy a home of their own on a small plot of land. It was a two-bedroom, one-bathroom house with a car port. All of the furniture in it was donated by our church, except for my bedroom set brought over from the Bowdens.

Since neither one of my birth parents spoke English, except sparsely, they needed someone to help them translate, write checks, etc. Neither one could drive a car, so Obigie rode his bicycle to work. Oma was picked up and dropped off by the women who employed her. Many of her employers were quite wealthy. Many of them also were the parents of my school classmates. I often felt embarrassed when my classmates found out Oma was their maid.

The Violations Continue

E.K. would come over to visit me at my parents' house. E.K. was always welcomed at the house. When he arrived Oma and Obigie would go outside to the garden and leave him alone in the house with me. As an adult, I look back on this ritual and realize they knew! They knew and didn't do anything to stop it!

I think they were so grateful that E.K. and my Mom had taken me to America that they didn't want to make any waves. They simply looked the other way and pretended the entire scenario was completely normal.

If I was inclined to give my birth parents the benefit of the doubt, I would say if they didn't know, they certainly practiced poor judgment. This is why I'm writing this down. I want people to realize that it doesn't take a lot of time to molest a child. Don't leave your kids alone with someone. If they say, "I don't like so-and-so," you should listen to them. They just may have a good reason. They may not be able to tell you why they don't like someone, probably because they were told to stay quiet. It's up to you to listen to them and honor their concerns.

Life with my Birth Family

Oma started a garden at home. She grew Asian peppers, melons, Korean radishes, and Korean water parsley. (She had smuggled the seeds into the US inside the lining of her clothes.) Oma sold her harvest in Killeen, Texas at the Asian markets. Mom would drive the food to the markets. I always assumed she took a cut.

Oma and Obigie would make rice cakes and mandoo (Korean pot-stickers). They also gathered acorns to make acorn powder for acorn jelly, a type of rice cake, and edible weeds to use as food coloring.

Oma also grew Korean cabbage and made kimchi with it (spicy, pickled cabbage).

This was all such a culture shock for me since E.K. shunned all things Korean. He taught me that Koreans were lazy. He said we weren't allowed to speak Korean in his home. He forbade Korean cooking. As an adult, I now view my birth parents as industrious, hard working, and dedicated. As a child, though, headed toward my teenage years, I was embarrassed by them.

My oldest brother was the last member of the family to come to the US. My parents were the ones who sponsored him. He was 27 when he arrived. He converted the carport at my parents' house into a third bedroom for himself and went to work in construction with E.K. He also bought me my first new coat. I got rid an old, ugly blue one I wore since I had lived with E.K. The kids at school often made fun of that coat.

My brother's fiancée came a year after his arrival. My parents didn't like her. My brother and his fiancée eventually moved to Chicago and opened a clothing store in a depressed neighborhood on Halstead Avenue. My family was scattered once again.

Meanwhile, I continued to visit my sister in Galveston during the summers. She had an American boyfriend named Steve. They would bribe me to get out of the apartment, so they could have some time alone. They'd give me $1.50 to get lost and then they would take me out to eat afterward. Sometimes, they would buy several pounds of fruit and we would split it. When my sister went to work I would eat her half, too! They actually let me get away with it! I was a brat, but I was also allowed to be a child during the summers. For the first time in my life, I was the child I was supposed to be!

Food is Love

I turned to food when I was bored and when I was lonely. Food became comfort, but it also became a problem for me later in my life. It may have started with eating as much fruit as I wanted while I was visiting my sister, but it extended to dinners at my mother's house. She would find one thing that I liked and would make it over and over and over again until I could no longer stand it. That's when I learned to cook for myself. I also learned to bake cookies and cakes. I started a lifelong habit of seeking American comfort food.

4

Another Transition

My sister got married on my 14th birthday. She had a fever of 104 degrees and was very sick that day, but went ahead with the wedding anyway. It turns out she had endocarditis, an inflammation of the lining of the heart. She spent a month in the hospital and almost died.

About a week before her wedding, I told her I didn't like her fiancee'. He had made a pass at me in the car and I told her about that. She completely disregarded me and he belittled me saying the "kiss" he wanted was not sexual in nature. I felt dirty, disrespected, and violated......again.

Off to Another House and Another Uncle

After my sister's wedding, I no longer went to visit her in Galveston. Now I was farmed off to E.K.'s sister's house for the summer. Her husband was an elder in a Pentecostal Church. This was my first experience with this type of church. This uncle brought us to church frequently. I often babysat the children at the church while services were going on.

My aunt and uncle owned an insurance company. Sometimes, he would come home while she was still at the office. A few times, he came into my bedroom and would say "come over here, I want to give you a hug." While he was giving me a hug he was looking down my shirt. He also fondled me through my shirt. I was shocked and humiliated. Once again I was told, "don't tell anyone; this is "Our Little Secret."

Food as Control

I decided to make my uncle 'pay' for his behavior. Since my aunt worked a lot, she didn't cook a lot, and we often went out to eat. I would make my uncle buy me dessert every single time, just to get back at him by making him spend more money.

Doreen Virtue writes in Constant Cravings: What your Food Cravings Mean that craving sweets is an "emotional hunger." Sweets, for me, became my great escape, and my "go-to" solution when I was feeling blue, depressed, or stressed. Sweets also became my "go to" for celebrations, happy events, and assorted life's pleasures. With this 'food culture' that I created for myself, it's easy to see how my weight would later become an issue.

I also used food to make myself unattractive. I figured if I were fat, people wouldn't look at me and if they didn't look at me, they wouldn't use and abuse me. This concept is well documented in the field of psychology. Margarita Tartakovsky, M.S. writes in her article "Wearing Your Weight As Armor" on PsychCentral.com:

> For individuals who've experienced a traumatic event, usually some kind of abuse, their weight helps them create a barrier to the outside.
>
> For some, weight serves to minimize their looks and sexuality. In today's society, thin is in, and if you don't fit the mold, in theory, people will pay less attention to you and your body. Some women use their weight as protection against future abuse.

According to the organization Survivors of Incest Anonymous:

> We perceive obesity to be unattractive, and if we believe or were told that we were abused because we were attractive, we may overeat in a misguided yet totally understandable attempt to defend ourselves from further sexual assault.

On his website, Michael D. Myers, M.D., an obesity and eating disorder specialist, estimates that 40 percent of his significantly obese patients have experienced sexual abuse (see http://psychcentral.com/blog/archives/2009/09/03/wearing-your-weight-as-armor/).

Myself at 16 years old and Warren Wooten.

Teenage Years

At age 11 I started getting my period. So by the time I was a teenager I was ahead of most of the other girls my age. Even though I was able to get pregnant, E.K. always reminded me "don't worry, you won't get pregnant; I shoot blanks." It wasn't until I was old to enough to fully understand what this meant that I realized why he never had children of his own. I also realized that this was why he thought it was "Okay" to violate me, because, as long as I didn't "tell," and since I wasn't going to get pregnant, there was no way he would ever get caught.

I was looking for love and affection from a father. I didn't respect Obigie or E.K. Obigie never had a backbone to stand up to Oma who ruled the roost. E.K. was a rapist, a bigot, and a hypocrite. It was at this time that I started to get into relationships with boys who were much older than I was. I was able to "give myself" to them because my virginity was already gone. I used sex as a commodity.

At age 14, I had a boyfriend who was 18. Other boyfriends were just a couple of years older than me, but none were my own age. By the time I was 16 and 17, I was dating men in their 20's. At 17, I dated Tom. He was the first boyfriend I told about my sexual abuse. He actually confronted E.K. about it. This was the first time someone wanted to protect me. Whatever he said, it must have worked, because E.K.

left me alone, at least for a while. My mom, on the other hand, said that I "brought shame to the family" by telling Tom.

Tom's parents came to Texas to meet my parents. They knew Tom was serious about me. They also wanted permission to take me with them to Ohio to attend a family wedding. They took my entire extended family out to dinner: both sets of parents, my sister and her husband, and my brother Jin and my brother Dae and his wife. During dinner, Tom's parents explained that they would act as chaperones at the family wedding and cover all expenses. Still, my parents said "no." I was devastated. I was so upset I wanted to kill myself. I said "I'm never going to get out of this place!"

Becoming an Adult

On my 18th birthday, I broke up with Tom. My family, who I still hoped against all hope actually cared about me, had said Tom was "dumb." Tom may not have been a genius, but he was a really good guy. I let my family talk me out of what might have been a lifelong relationship built on love and honesty. Those qualities had been sorely lacking in my life. I am truly sorry, even to this day, about the way I treated Tom.

At 18, I started dating my cousin's brother-in-law, Doug, whom I met when we were both part of my cousin's wedding party. It was during this time that I realized my cousin had an inkling about my childhood trauma. After about three weeks of dating, I told Doug there was something I wanted him to know about my childhood. Once I told him about the incest, he said he already knew, that my cousin had already told him about it. I was shocked! I realized my family, even my extended family, knew all along and did nothing to protect me. I was betrayed yet again. I was sad. Maybe I should have been angry, but I was just so sad. Even to this day, I am sad about it. I dated Doug three months, then I broke up with him.

One day while I was at the University of Texas, my mom showed up. She told me E.K. had hit her. She told me that she was going to divorce him. I was glad. I told her I would testify in court about all the abuse I had suffered and still continued to suffer. E.K. had been coming to my college apartment and had been propositioning me. When mom heard this she decided to go back and tell him she was leaving him and filing for divorce. About an hour and a half later, she called me and said "I'm a good Christian woman. He asked me for forgiveness, and I gave it to him." I hung up on her.

I went to my friend Matt's dorm room and sobbed uncontrollably. I told him I needed some help, maybe some psychological counseling. I called my sister from Matt's room and the two of them talked me out of counseling. She said "You're a smart girl; you have all these people who love you. You don't need to go and get help." Matt agreed.

I dated Matt off and on for nine years. It was a very destructive relationship; very bad for my self-esteem. When he went home on the first summer vacation, he never answered any of my 27 letters. When he came back in the fall, he thought we would pick up right where we left off. Eventually, he wore me down and we started dating again. This was an unhealthy relationship, albeit a lengthy one. When he went to medical school, years later, he said he couldn't get through school if I left him. He said he would kill himself if I didn't continue the relationship. I believed him. I stayed with him. Matt, it turns out, was cheating on me, all the while professing how he couldn't live without me. When I learned about this I broke up with Matt.

Asserting Independence

At age 18, I no longer felt compelled to be dependent on "parents," so I started to explore new experiences and learn who I really was. I made friends with gay men because they were fun and because they posed no threat to me. This helped shatter my strict Christian upbringing. I also dated Matt, who was Jewish. Straying outside of my faith was a major step for me.

I studied comparative religion in college, and learned that many of the teachings I was brought up with were either immovable or simply too strident for me. Fundamentalism was no longer in my comfort zone. I also had no stomach for proselytizing.

I started volunteering at People's Community Clinic in Austin, Texas, which served primarily people who did not have any healthcare. I learned to take blood pressure, temperature, weight and height; all of the things that are standard in an initial exam. The real need at the clinic, though, was fitting women with diaphragms. I learned how to do this and the doctors would come in and check to make sure the fit was correct.

I had to become very comfortable in learning female anatomy. I also learned to have a calm, professional bedside manner made an uncomfortable situation for most patients less unsettling. I believe this experience helped me to develop the skills I use to this day when I talk with women about sexuality. I also believe it helped me develop the proper demeanor in my current profession as a massage therapist and healer.

I also learned about all of the forms of birth control and the statistics associated with each method so I could teach patients. I discussed the risks of STD's, especially with multiple partners. Herpes was a major concern in those days. AIDS was still in its infancy, but I knew people who had it, some of whom had died.

According to the CDC, the AIDS epidemic officially began on June 5, 1981, as cited in its "Morbidity and Mortality Weekly Report."

I learned to figure out my own morality and ethics. During this time in my life, I also started to explore religions to find my 'truth.' In addition, I learned not to judge other people's lifestyles. "Love is love," was becoming a big thing in the '80's and is again today. I was expanding my horizons through my associations with many different kinds of people; this was something that was not encouraged or ever experienced when I was a child.

Soomi (step niece), Yong (Mom), myself at 24 years old, my Oma, and Joyce (niece) in Washington D.C. 1986.

5

Meeting Brian

It was time to move on. I was tired of Texas; I was tired of my relationship with Matt, and I wanted to see if the relationship could withstand the stress of long distance. I wanted to forge my own identity, so I moved to Indianapolis to attend Indiana University where I studied business and then political science.

While I was a full-time student I had a great physician on campus. She told me about a place called the Julian Center. The center provided counseling with payment on a sliding scale so I could actually afford it! The Julian Center was founded to provide services to victims of domestic violence, sexual assault, and other crises. For the first time in my life I was able to get the formal counseling I sorely needed. My therapist, Windy, worked with me for quite some time. When she left to go into private practice, she gave me the opportunity to continue our therapy. We met for two hours a week.

My biggest transformation was that I lost 30 pounds in a month! I believe it was my ability to finally express and let go of my shame and guilt that helped me do this. Letting go of my toxic emotions helped me to shed my toxic pounds. At the same time I was finding my voice through counseling, I was finding my voice through school. I became involved in school politics as a representative of the School of Business.

I served on the Search and Screen Committee to select a new Dean of Student Affairs. During this time I learned the current dean had a conflict of interest: she was serving in the dual role as assistant dean of faculty. With this in mind I believed the best way to make changes was to run for Student Body President. I lost, because the current dean declared the election null and void. I learned once again through this experience that life is not fair. Power can slap you down, but you just have to find a way to get up again.

During my last year at the university, I had to take a rhetoric class in order to graduate. I was 27 years old. I was in the same class as a bunch of freshmen students from provincial neighborhoods of Indiana. I stuck out like a sore thumb. Brian was in that class. He was one of the best writers and speakers there. We all had to choose partners for the class so I chose Brian. Even though he was six-and-a-half years younger than me, he seemed older than his years when compared to the other students. I recognized him as being an "old soul." When he brought me a copy of The Unbearable Lightness of Being by Milan Kundera, I looked at him, not for his age, but for his incredible sensitivity. It seemed that he, too, was searching for his voice in life.

We knew each other for just one semester when Brian told me he was in love with me. He said he would follow me to Washington, D.C., where I was going to use my degree in political science. I wanted to change the world, to work on civil rights and women's rights. D.C. was the place to be.

Since I didn't have a trust fund, and I didn't have an actual job either, I went to interview at the Four Seasons Hotel in Georgetown until my great PoliSci job could come through. I got a job at the Four Seasons as Room Service Coordinator. Sometimes I was the coat check girl, which by the way, was very lucrative. People were generous tippers!

I wanted to transfer to another department because I wasn't very happy working for the room service manager. I transferred to the fitness club. It was 1990. We had the first-ever luxury hotel fitness club that included private memberships. The manager said if I went to massage school, at my own expense, they would employ me at the Four Seasons. That's how it all began!

The Four Seasons taught me about customer service,

about meeting people's needs, and about problem solving. People literally came to the fitness club and told me I was so friendly and so helpful that they felt I would "exercise for them" if I could!

Brian interviewed for the job of overnight bellboy. He declined the job. He had no idea how much money he left on the table! He also decided to go back to Indiana to finish school. This decision was effectively a break-up. By this time, I was working 70 hours a week, splitting my time between the fitness club and helping out with room service. I hardly ever saw Brian anyway.

6

While I was working at the Four Seasons I met many interesting and famous people. One of my first massage clients became a princess. Really! I gave her a massage, she went to a party in the evening, and I gave her a massage the next day. It's then that she told me "I met my prince." I said, "that's very nice!" She said, "No, really, I met my prince at the party!" She introduced me to her future father-in-law. She recommended he come see me for a massage. He was the king of Greece! His son, the prince, later married my client.

The king (deposed, by the way) told me it was okay if I mentioned him as a royal recommendation. He introduced me to several other current and former royalty from several countries who also became my clients. In the interest of client confidentiality, I won't mention them here, but the list is long and varied and includes movie stars, rock stars, leaders of Fortune 500 companies, international CEOs and heads of state. The Four Seasons was my connection to all of these people.

My Birth Parents

In 1992, Oma and Obigie, my birth parents, moved in with me in Rosslyn, Virginia. They said they did so because my brother and sister "didn't need them" for babysitting anymore. Of course, I didn't need a babysitter at that time either, but I believed I should keep the family together because I wanted to heal the family wounds. I vowed to stick by Oma and Obigie even though they didn't stick by me.

Transformation

I started doing my first "transformational workshop" in 1992 after my break-up with Brian. It was a program called "LifeSpring." It was part of a number of human potential workshops that were popular at the time. Some of the courses I took included: sexuality, family, basic, advanced and masters. I also took leadership training. My family and friends joined me in these workshops including my sister, my niece, my brother, and my two sisters-in-law. The process brought my family together, but it also exposed many of the fractures within the family dynamic. Since we were still in touch, I tried to enroll Brian in these courses. He resisted.

In 1994, my sister left her husband and moved to Virginia with her daughter. We all moved in together: My sister, my Oma and Obigie, my niece and myself. I started working as a freelance massage therapist to several luxury hotels in Washington, D.C. Concierges of these hotels would call me when they had a V.I.P. in town because they knew I would provide V.I.P. service.

Reconnecting with Brian

In a roundabout way, it was the Grateful Dead that brought Brian and I back together. Over the years, the band had stayed at the Four Seasons and the members heard about me. They hired me to work on them before and after a concert at RFK Stadium in Washington, D.C. Then, I was asked to meet them in Indiana for the next stop on their tour.

I went to Indiana for the concert. I could see Jerry Garcia was not looking well. The venue was small, the music was 'off' that night, and people seemed to be on edge. There was extra drama when fans who were unable to get into the concert toppled a fence and stormed the venue. It was chaos. The show was stopped mid-concert.

I was supposed to work on the band members the next day but when I called the hotel, drummer Bill

Kreutzmann told me the band was getting a police escort to the airport. After the previous night, the band's safety was a concern and the police weren't taking any chances, so the job was off.

Since I was already in Indianapolis, I asked Brian to meet with me. We met at a bar called Union Jack's in a neighborhood called Broad Ripple. We discussed what had happened in our relationship. we cleared up misunderstandings. We decided to try again.

I told him if we were going to get back together, he would have to take a transformational workshop-type course. He agreed that we would do a workshop together called the Hoffman Process. Normally, couples are not permitted to take this course together but since Brian and I were just considering restarting our relationship again, they allowed us to join with one condition: that we would not interfere with each other's 'processes' for the first five days. In addition, clear boundaries were set by separating us into different working groups.

For the first time in my life, at the age of 33, I felt completely integrated thanks to the Hoffman Process. The workshop brings together your physical Body, your Intellect (mind), your Spiritual Self and your Emotional Child. It helps you to go through anger and grief until you arrive at a place of understanding, compassion, and forgiveness. This allows you to love again (see www.hoffmaninstitute.org).

Later, my sister and I bought a house together in Fairfax, Virginia; the entire extended family including my boyfriend, Brian, all lived there together. It took about a year, but the extended family became a bit too much for me and Brian so we moved to our own place. My sister, niece, and parents remained in the house.

Brian and myself September 1995 at the Hoffman Process re-birthday.

7

Marriage

Brian and I got married in 1996. We eloped to Las Vegas because I didn't want my parents to force me to have my wedding at a Korean church. We also didn't want Brian's parents to impose their wishes on us. Instead, we were married in a civil ceremony.

We invited family and friends several months later to attend a "Public Promise" ceremony at the Park Hyatt Hotel in Georgetown in Washington, D.C.. My niece played Pachelbel's Canon in D on the violin. My other niece played the piano. We also had a Korean opera singer whom my mother imposed upon me at the last minute. She had a beautiful voice. It could have been a disaster but it wasn't. The ceremony was followed by a "Queen's High Tea" reception: pastries and finger sandwiches. About 80 people attended.

Brian and I enjoying the Public Promise (our mock wedding).

David Jung (nephew), Joyce Choi (niece) on the violin, my sister Elizabeth, and Cathy Jung on the piano. They performed Pachelbel's Canon in D during the wedding reception.

Korean opera singer (woman in foreground) my Oma imposed on me on the day of the Public Promise.

Making Peace

In 1997, I visited with E.K. I told him I forgave him. He told me he was sorry. I truly believe that he said he was sorry because he wanted something from me: He wanted me to promise I would take care of mom if anything happened to him. At the time I accepted his apology. In retrospect, I do not believe he was sorry at all.

I did not see E.K. again until almost 19 years later. I did speak to him on the phone until I was 50 although I found it increasingly difficult and painful. Eventually, I stopped speaking to him for almost four years. At the age of 50 years old, I finally gave myself permission not to call my family on holidays. I was able to let go of the guilt I had placed on myself to be the "good daughter" and a "good spiritual person." I realized I didn't have to listen to any of my parents any more. It was too draining, and I was old enough to make my own decisions about my own life. I learned to set healthy boundaries.

Starting a Family

In 1999 I left my job as a massage therapist at the Four Seasons Hotel to start my own spa. I was 38 and I also decided it was time to start my own family. I worked with a business consultant who convinced me to start a family first; she advised me that I could start my own spa at any time, but starting my own family was another matter. I followed her advice.

In 2000, my son Cameron was born in the year of the Golden Dragon. I was 38. Oma became Cameron's baby sitter. I was able to go back to work part time. I worked as a massage therapist for "Sports Club LA."

In 2003, my son Sean was born in the year of the Goat. I was 41. Oma picked up babysitting responsibilities for Sean and Cameron. Oma and Obigie moved from their house to an apartment in Arlington, Virginia in 2005. Obigie was so happy to move into the apartment complex! It was a senior community that included 20 other Korean families! They had activities right there and didn't have to depend upon anyone to drive them anywhere. Everything was nearby.

Oma, on the other hand, wasn't so happy. She wanted to continue to live with us, but Brian and I decided we needed to create 'healthy boundaries,' and live a life of our own. We eased my parents into the transition by having them stay with us part time at first, and then full time on their own.

Brian, myself, Cameron, and Sean 2003.

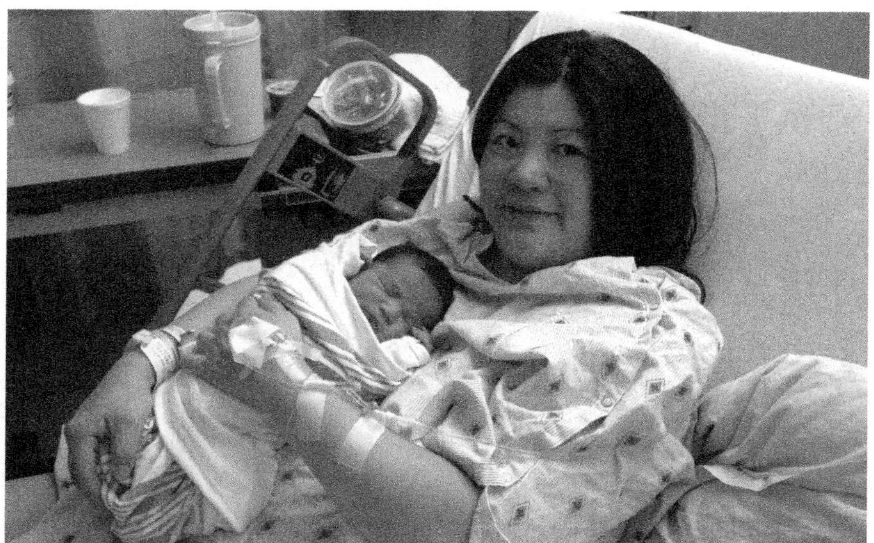

Myself with Cameron August 28, 2000.

Christmas 2012. Sean, Cameron, myself, and Brian.

Three generations of Martin men Easter 2017. Ed (Brian's Dad), Sean, Cameron, and Brian.

Starting my "Be You Spa"

In 2005, I started looking for locations for the spa I have hoped to start almost six years earlier. I created a holistic center with retail products including skin care, essential oils and books. We had workshops and exercise classes. I also did therapeutic massage and facials. The spa was originally named "Be You Bi You Wellness Center and Spa." I later changed it to "Be You Spa."

Brian's Illness

A year after I opened my spa, my husband was hospitalized due to an infection that began with a tiny scrape on his elbow. One day after the scrape occurred,

I noticed his elbow was inflamed. His doctor prescribed a treatment with Z-Pak, an antibiotic treatment that uses azithromycin over the course of several days. He started it on a Sunday. On Monday, he came down with what he thought was the flu. On Tuesday, he spent the entire day in bed. On Wednesday morning, he nearly passed out. I took him to the emergency room.

The nearest hospital was Reston Hospital Center in Reston, Virginia. Brian was given an IV of antibiotics and was told he had cellulitis. He was sent home and told to come back the next day for another round of IV antibiotics. Before he left, the doctor used a marker and drew a circle around the inflamed area on Brian's elbow. When he came back the next day, the area had more than tripled. That's when the doctors realized something much more serious was going on.

Brian's father had given us a loan just before this happened. We used it to pay the six thousand dollars we owed on our health insurance and to reinstate our lapsed coverage. If we had not had the foresight to do this we would have been wiped out financially. Brian underwent surgery. He spent the next two days under quarantine in the intensive care unit for treatment of necrotizing fasciitis. This is widely known as "flesh eating bacteria," a potentially fatal infection.

Brian was moved to a private room after his first surgery and remained under quarantine for several more days. He was discharged after a total of three surgeries which included two debridements to remove the dead tissue in Brian's arm and one hand surgery: a bilateral carpal tunnel release to relieve nerve impingement caused by the swelling from a Group A Streptococcus, the strain of "flesh-eating bacteria" that was responsible for the infection.

Brian's health was in a fragile state. His father and my sister were at the hospital with him. I had to make a difficult choice to go to the hospital or to the spa. A celebration had previously been planned and was already set up to mark the one-year anniversary of the grand-opening. I decided to send my two little boys, ages 6 and 3 with their babysitter to see Brian at the hospital. I was in anguish over the realization that this could have been the last time they would ever see their father.

In the end, I made the heart-wrenching decision to go to the spa and see clients and help out with the celebration. I felt such angst in doing so but I also realized that I was providing the only income for the family and had to swallow my pain and go forward.

Brian could have lost his arm. He could have lost his life. The entire experience was so traumatic it caused me to relapse into a fear-survival mode. I was functional until about six months later at which time I experienced symptoms of severe post-traumatic stress. I had been dealing with Brian's illness, the financial burdens of his healthcare, and the burdens of keeping my spa and my family afloat.

Brian recovered about six months later with full use of his arm and hand. Still, he was not out of the woods. He sank into a deep depression. In addition, the 2008 financial collapse affected our livelihood and our home. We tried to renegotiate the mortgage on our house, and we had to give up the spa and file for personal bankruptcy. In 2009, the debts were discharged under bankruptcy law provisions. In 2010 our house went into foreclosure after we were unable to renegotiate our loan. We moved out in 2011 and went to Maryland where we started anew.

It was not until 2012, when I realized I needed help for my own depression. The accumulation of stress and trauma set me backward. I reverted to that child within who felt shame and humiliation. I needed to come back, to get out of my depression, to do what I called my "final work." I went through a combination of traditional therapy and healing techniques that helped pull me out of it.

8

Transition

During the 11 years they lived on their own in the apartment, it became clear that Oma and Obigie needed more help. Oma steadfastly refused to accept any help at all. She was convinced that she was able to care for herself and Obigie. I was dealing with Oma's depression and my father's overall decline.

The Phone Call

In March of 2015 my brother Jin called me to berate me for not staying in touch with the family especially, E.K. and Yong (mom). He told me Yong was in a nursing home. He urged me to call and check on her. I said "Jin! I am dealing with my own problems here! Our real parents are in serious decline and it's all falling on my shoulders!" Jin persisted saying I had to call E.K. and I lost it. I said "Jin, when I was nine years old,

E.K. raped me!" Jin, as if he didn't hear me, blurted out "He raped you?"

This is the hardest part of it. He lived in the same house, and he either didn't fully understand what incest was all about, or he was in deep denial about it. I think this speaks volumes about the misunderstanding about incest; people don't seem to acknowledge or comprehend that incest is rape.

Incest is a nebulous term that distances you from the horror and the abuse. It gives your family members "cover." It perpetuates the silence. It pressures victims to "keep quiet" and "act normal" and to continue the lie about what normalcy really is. The wound keeps getting bigger. No one wants to talk about what really happened. They want to sweep it under the rug. They don't want to deal with the consequences.

Interventions

One day when they were at their community center, the caseworker for the building called me and said "your father smells like urine." I asked the caseworker to put Oma on the phone and I told her, in Korean (which I can only spell phonetically) "ojem namseh suh Obigie" which means "father smells like he urinated." I also told her to give him a bath. She said "okay." When the caseworker came back on the phone, she said "by the way, your mother smells like urine too."

I asked Oma for the phone number of the Korean caregiver. I called her and set up an appointment to meet her at Oma and Obigie's apartment the very next day so we could have an "intervention." I knew my Korean language skills weren't going to be enough to handle the complex nuances and emotions that were sure to erupt so I asked the Korean caregiver to be there to translate.

Through the translator I told Oma I love her but I cannot be there 24-7 and I'm trying to find a solution to get her and Obigie some help so they could continue to live on their own. I told her if she wouldn't agree to do this, Obigie would have to go to the nursing home and so would she. I explained that in a nursing home they would have no control over anything in their lives; also, there would be no guarantee of a Korean community. I firmly explained that she needed to cooperate and allow caregivers into the apartment, or the nursing home would be their only option. The manager of the apartment complex, who was also at the intervention, concurred.

Oma's response, translated from Korean, was "I'm going to poison your father, then I"m going to poison myself, and you won't have to worry about us." I knew she was angry, and maybe a bit frightened, but her defiant response was only making things worse.

Two more interventions later, Oma agreed to accept help in the apartment. We finally found someone

Oma and Obijie at his 60th birthday in 1980.

Obijie at 99, and Oma at 89 in February 2016.

she was comfortable with. She was a young Korean woman with three children. Sometimes, the caregiver would bring her three year old daughter with her. Oma bonded with this little girl. I could not help but make the mental note, tinged with a stab of pain, that three was my exact age when I was given up for adoption.

Some four months after the caregiver started coming, Oma called me. It was a Sunday. She said she and Obigie didn't go to church. It was a big deal for them to miss church so I instantly knew something was terribly wrong. I rushed to their apartment and saw Obigie laying on the floor. I called 911. The ambulance took him (Obigie) to the hospital and I followed behind in my car. By the time the caregiver and I were allowed into the examining room, Oma and Obigie were hopelessly confused and agitated.

Obigie was taken to have a CatScan and doctors determined he had suffered a form of stroke called a brain bleed. Given his age and condition there were no options other than to make him comfortable until hospice care could be arranged.

I called all my siblings. My brother Jin saw my Facebook post that said I was at the hospital with Obigie so he called me before I had a chance to call him. His voice sounded strange and weak. I asked why and he said he was in the hospital recovering from gall bladder surgery and had developed complications. I told him Obigie was dying and said I would keep him informed; in the meantime I urged him to concentrate on his own health. I called my other brother Dae and informed him about what was going on.

I stayed with Obigie in the hospital for two and a half straight days, until he was discharged to home hospice care. I knew he didn't have much time left, so I asked my husband to bring the boys to come see him. By the time they got there, Obigie would not wake up. They never got to see him coherent again. He died at home seven days later at 4am, March 22nd, 2016. San Bong Jung, "Obigie," was 96.

I wrote this on the day he died:

> He lived a wonderful life of faith, family and kindness. He loved to laugh and have fun. His last joke was to my mother in the hospital ER room. She asked if he was sleeping. He was facing her and said "How can I sleep when I can look at your beautiful face."

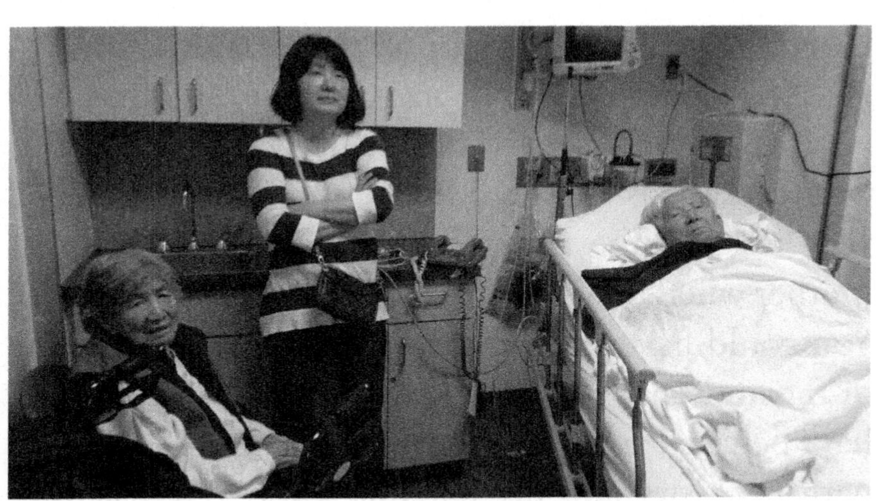

Oma, Obijie's caregiver, and Obijie at the ER March 6, 2016.

9

Funeral Drama

My brother's 60th birthday was the same day as Obigie's funeral service, Good Friday. It was a long day of family togetherness, a mix of muted joy and barely contained sadness. First we celebrated birth (my brother Jin's) and then, that evening, we honored Obigie at his funeral. I delivered the eulogy at the funeral service. Here is part of what I said:

"Nae edemon Hyun Ju-ao." (My name is Hyun Ju). Na Inchon jum wasayo (I came from Inchon). Those were the words I learned in the summer of my 10th year as I became reacquainted with my father and mother when they came to the US from South Korea. You could have put any two Korean people in front of me and said 'these are your parents,' and I would have believed you. That summer I spent in Galveston with my sister and my parents. They were teaching

My brother Jin at his 60th birthday celebration.

Myself, Cameron, Sean, Brian, Oma, and Jin at his 60th birthday celebration.

me Korean because I had forgotten it. My father was trying to teach me to be proud of being Korean. I learned a lot from him."

My eulogy was the first time the congregation and the minister learned the story of my family. The minister later told me this was the first time he understood the family dynamics. He never could figure out until he heard the eulogy why I didn't speak Korean. He didn't know that the oldest children were not around (which is very unusual in Asian culture) and he didn't understand why the youngest daughter (me) didn't speak the language.

The next day, the day of my father's burial service, my sister and oldest brother Dae were sitting on a couch in the funeral home. As I walked in my sister said, "Hyun Ju: Dae and I decided when Oma dies, we're going to cremate her and spread her ashes over Obigie."

I was shocked. First of all, I told her "this is not the time to talk about this and no, you will not do that." I reminded her that cremation would go against Oma's wishes and I walked away. I told my brother Jin and he agreed with me that Oma would not want that.

After the funeral, Dae didn't even stay to have lunch with us. He said he had to go back to Ohio so he could go to sunrise Easter Service. He chose this over spending even one more day with the family. My sister and I took Oma to Easter service, in part, out of respect for her, and in part to thank all of the people who had come to my father's funeral.

Mom On Her Own

After nearly 70 years of marriage Oma was alone. She was lost, confused and probably in shock. People in the apartment complex began to come to visit her daily and the caregiver still comes every day. Sometimes, the caregiver takes Oma to stay at her house because Oma says she's so very lonely. I go to see her at least once a week. While Oma gets plenty of attention during the day, her evenings are difficult; this is when she is most lonely without Obigie.

Talking to My Adoptive Parents

I hadn't spoken to Yong (mom) and E.K. for years and certainly didn't feel like it now, but my brother Jin convinced me I should tell them about Obigie's death. I reluctantly agreed to make the call, even though I knew it was going to be very difficult. Yong answered the phone. I said, "This is Hyun." She said, "who is this?" I said "it's Hyun, Mom."

She was still confused and put E.K. on the phone. He was the last person in the universe I wanted to talk to but he immediately recognized my voice. I said, "I just wanted to call and let you know that Obigie,

Myself and Oma at Obijie's grave 2016.

Dad and Mom at their house in Lampasas, Texas 2016.

died today." E.K. blurted out, "We can't come (to the funeral). We're sick and we're broke." "I don't expect you to come," I said. "I am just making this phone call to let you know Obigie is dead."

E.K. continued to talk about why they weren't coming to the funeral but I stopped listening. I had done my part, I said what I needed to say and then I said goodbye. I told my brother Jin about the phone call and said "don't ever make me do this again. It really hurts me and causes such a drain of energy."

It was because of that phone call that we decided Jin would be the one to call them again; this time to make plans for their eventual funerals. We wanted to handle the situation better than we had handled my Obigie's funeral. We knew the first thing we had to do was get the legal Power of Attorney and Medical Directive. Jin was going to be the P.O.A., not me; but I coached him through the call. We got mom to agree to allow Jin to assume the responsibility.

Intervention and Confrontation

A month after Obigie's funeral, Jin flew out to Lampasas, Texas. He was still battling health problems of his own. I later learned he was suffering from cancer. Surgeons discovered it when they performed his gall bladder surgery. While he had alluded to 'complications' at the time, I had no idea that he was talking about cancer.

During Obigie's funeral Jin had stayed with me and we spoke at length about our childhood, our siblings and about the abuse. By the end of his trip, Jin was able to acknowledge that he, too, had been victimized by our adoptive parents. He finally acknowledged, some 35 years later, that he was sorry for telling me when I was 18 years old to just let it go, to forget about it, when I told him about the sexual abuse.

I let him know that it really hurt that I was basically told to "be quiet," just like mom had told me throughout my childhood. Jin realized HE had been "quiet" as well; he had repressed his OWN anger at being used by these people who adopted us as their personal slaves. Jin was forced to do all of the chores. Among other things, he had to muck out the stalls, exercise the horses, milk the cows and clean out the chicken coop. I was forced to be E.K.'s sexual slave and housemaid.

When he set out for his visit to Texas to talk to mom and E.K. he was under the impression that my two boys were going to be the beneficiaries of their Will. When Jin got there he was confronted with much more than he had bargained for. He found mom in a confused and zombie-like state. E.K. was argumentative, confrontational and made racial comments. Jin called me for emotional support. He was already dealing with his his own health problems and he found this experience to be emotionally taxing and destructive.

Jin managed to secure the legal Power of Attorney, but he needed a notary and a witness to sign the document. The next door neighbor was a notary and was very helpful during the whole process of getting both the Power of Attorney and the Medical Directive. Jin also went to the bank where he was officially added to the bank accounts as a signatory.

When he got back to the house he asked about the Will. Jin found mom and EK to be evasive. So he said, "Just give me the gist of it, if you don't have a copy." That's when he found out he and I each were to get a total of one-thousand dollars. The rest was to go to my cousin, Chong Kyun, who lives in Texas. Jin blew his stack. He said, "You abused Hyun sexually, you beat me and made me work as your slave!"

He later told me he blasted them for about 20 minutes as he let go of all of his pent-up anger and frustration. His outburst made an impression. Mom came out of her normal "zombie-state" and started crying. She apologized to him. She insisted she didn't know what had happened to me and Jin.

Jin left the house and drove to the WalMart parking lot. He was pumped. He said he just had to get out of there. In an almost manic state, built upon the foundation of a lifetime of repression, he told me everything. He also said he thought I should talk to mom and that it would be "healing" for both of us.

I gave him permission to call me when he went back to the house and agreed to speak to them.

Final Thoughts

Jin called me about 15 minutes later. He said, "I'm giving the phone to mom. When she got on the phone she said "I didn't know! Why didn't you tell me when you were five?" "I DID tell you when I was 12." I reminded her I didn't tell her at five because I was told to "be quiet" and I didn't want to be punished. "When I was 12," I said, "and I DID tell you, you said "Don't tell anybody, and if it happens again it's your fault." She just cried and said "I'm sorry." She kept repeating "I didn't know."

I added "When I was 18, I told you again, after he hit you. You told me at that time you were going to divorce E.K. I said I would testify against him during divorce proceedings and you would get everything! You went back to his house, called me and said 'I am a good Christian woman. I forgave him.' That broke my heart. It really did."

Through tear-filled gasps, she added "I want to see you and your kids! I want you to come and bring Cameron and Sean. I haven't seen them!" She has never met them because I made the deliberate decision to protect them from that toxic side of the family. And although it wasn't my goal, my decision had hurt her.

I said, “I love you. I forgive you.” I did not commit to visit or to bring my children so she could see them.

I realized “Mom” is a prisoner in her own home. EK has always made her feel small, insignificant, unimportant. She was no longer the beautiful young woman who committed to marriage so many years ago to a man, it turns out, she did not really know.

Jin took the phone as “mom” continued to cry. He said, “do you want to confront E.K?” Before I could answer, E.K. came on the phone. He said “This is E.K! Hyun Ju, why are you tellin’ these lies!” I said “I’m NOT telling lies! You DID do this to me! You started when I was five and you raped me when I was nine! And you kept trying to get ‘in my pants’ until I left Texas.” “Well I don’t remember any of that,” he said. “I’m glad you don’t,” I said, “but you did it!” E.K handed the phone back to Jin. Jin said “I’m sorry he doesn’t remember, and denies it, but mom believes you and I believe you.”

Despite health problems wearing him down. Jin left Texas feeling light on his feet, ten feet tall, and fully free after all these years! He realized he could stand up to E.K. in a way he was always afraid to do. He stood up for me, which he was always afraid to do, and he no longer had anything to fear from anyone or any thing.

Embraced and Integrated Child with Adult Self

By Hyun Martin

Robbed of my innocence and childhood
My adult self learns to listen and validate
My inner child screams, rages, and cries
At the injustice of abandonment, betrayal
And abuse of terror living with a blue-eyed
Monster named Dad.
Having a complicit Mom saying,
"Ke quiet! Don't bring shame to the family!
If it happens again, it's your fault!"

Having survived the rapes, the torture, the terror,
I learned to flee my body and split off into
My perfect world of my imagination
The pain, the grief, resignation to years
Of endless abuse and terror.

Now as an adult being still
I learn to hear the inner voice of my child within,
Comfort and embrace my child and say,
I feel your pain, rage and grief!
You can feel your feelings and I understand.

You are Safe!
You were born a perfect child!
You Survived!
You are Lovable!
You are Loved!
You are Love!
You are Innocent!
It is not your Fault!
It is not your Shame!
It is not your Guilt!
Your body was just reacting to a stimulus.
You are blameless!

Please grow with me to our physical age into an adult!
All the pieces of my soul, I get to gather,
glue and heal with gold and Light
For each break is worth noting, reclaiming the power
Of healing our collective heart!
Embracing the Imperfect and Knowing
I am Perfectly Imperfect!
Being and embracing me and creating the space for
You to Be You,
So I can Be Me!

My final thoughts are that I have been influenced by the ideals of the Kennedys. I hope to Be the change I want to see in the world. Like those who have gone before carrying the torch of Truth and Justice, I hope you will join in this journey of co-creating a world at Peace.

I'm only going to talk to you just for a minute or so this evening, because I have some -- some very sad news for all of you -- Could you lower those signs, please? -- I have some very sad news for all of you, and, I think, sad news for all of our fellow citizens, and people who love peace all over the world; and that is that Martin Luther King was shot and was killed tonight in Memphis, Tennessee.

Martin Luther King dedicated his life to love and to justice between fellow human beings. He died in the cause of that effort. In this difficult day, in this difficult time for the United States, it's perhaps well to ask what kind of a nation we are and what direction we want to move in. For those of you who are black -- considering the evidence evidently is that there were white people who were responsible -- you can be filled with bitterness, and with hatred, and a desire for revenge.

We can move in that direction as a country, in greater polarization -- black people amongst blacks, and white amongst whites, filled with hatred toward one another. Or we can make an effort, as Martin Luther King did, to understand, and to comprehend, and replace that violence, that stain of bloodshed that has spread across our land, with an effort to understand, compassion, and love.

For those of you who are black and are tempted to fill with -- be filled with hatred and mistrust of the injustice of such an act, against all white people, I would only say that I can also feel in my own heart the same kind of feeling. I had a member of my family killed, but he was killed by a white man.

But we have to make an effort in the United States. We have to make an effort to understand, to get beyond, or go beyond these rather difficult times.

My favorite poem, my -- my favorite poet was Aeschylus. And he once wrote:

Even in our sleep, pain which cannot forget
falls drop by drop upon the heart,
until, in our own despair,
against our will,
comes wisdom
through the awful grace of God.

What we need in the United States is not division; what we need in the United States is not hatred; what we need in the United States is not violence and lawlessness, but is love, and wisdom, and compassion toward one another, and a feeling of justice toward those who still suffer within our country, whether they be white or whether they be black.

So I ask you tonight to return home, to say a prayer for the family of Martin Luther King -- yeah, it's true -- but more importantly to say a prayer for our own country, which all of us love -- a prayer for understanding and that compassion of which I spoke.

We can do well in this country. We will have difficult times. We've had difficult times in the past, but we -- and we will have difficult times in the future. It is not the end of violence; it is not the end of lawlessness; and it's not the end of disorder.

But the vast majority of white people and the vast majority of black people in this country want to live together, want to improve the quality of our life, and want justice for all human beings that abide in our land.

And let's dedicate ourselves to what the Greeks wrote so many years ago: to tame the savageness of man and make gentle the life of this world. Let us dedicate ourselves to that, and say a prayer for our country and for our people.

Thank you very much.

—Robert F. Kennedy
Speech in Indianapolis, IN on April 4, 1968

My picture in The Women's March January 21, 2017

Standing for Women's and Children's Rights helps our society become a more just world. Protesting, speaking our truths to power, voting and exercising our minds and hearts for equality and respect for all people. Imagine a world of peace. Hugs and Blessings!

CPSIA information can be obtained
at www.ICGtesting.com
Printed in the USA
BVOW06s1350240717
489806BV00006B/32/P